Flamingos

Victoria Blakemore

Copyright info/picture credits

Cover, Jeff McGraw/AdobeStock; Page 3, skeeze/Pixabay; Page 5, Inichetti/AdobeStock; Page 7, pixel-mixer/Pixabay; Page 9, dimitrivetsikas1969/Pixabay; Pages 10-11, sunsinger/AdobeStock; Page 13, PDPics/Pixabay; Page 15, mejn/AdobeStock; Page 17, cynthiag/AdobeStock; Page 19, luc-theo/Pixabay; Page 21, jamiessg/Pixabay; Page 23; dejavu-designs/AdobeStock; Page 25, Antonio Jorge Nunes/AdobeStock; Page 27, mhskypixel/AdobeStock; Page 29, Curi-oso Photography/AdobeStock; Page 31, Matt/AdobeStock; Page 33, PatternPictures/Pixabay

Table of Contents

What Are Flamingos?

Flamingos are tall, pink birds with long legs and necks.

They can grow to be up to five feet tall with a **wingspan** of up to five feet wide.

Flamingos can be many shades
of pink.

Kinds of Flamingos

There are six different kinds of flamingos. They differ in their size, color, and where they live.

The greater flamingo is the most **widespread** flamingo.

There are more greater

flamingos than any other

kind.

Physical Characteristics

Flamingos have very long legs for their size. Their knees bend forwards instead of backwards like human knees. This lets them tuck their legs up under their body.

Their necks are very flexible and can curve in different directions. This lets them turn their head and **preen** feathers with their bill.

Habitat

Flamingos live in saltwater marshes, lakes, and lagoons. They usually prefer areas that are warm with lots of space.

Flamingos are able to **adapt** to different habitats as long as they have enough food.

Range

Flamingos can be found in Africa, Asia, Europe, North America, and South America.

Some kinds of flamingos **migrate** to different places at different times of the year.

Diet

Flamingos are **omnivores**.

They eat larva, bugs,

crustaceans, or small plants

like algae.

Their long necks let them

bend down and gather food

from the ground.

Flamingos strain mud and sand

through hair-like combs in their

bill.

Coloring

A red **pigment** called

carotene in their food is

what makes flamingo

feathers pink.

Without carotene, their

feathers would be white!

Flamingos that are healthy

usually have brightly colored

feathers.

Communication

Flamingos can growl, honk, and squawk to warn each other of danger.

They also use movement to communicate. They display their wings, march in groups, and move their heads to communicate with each other.

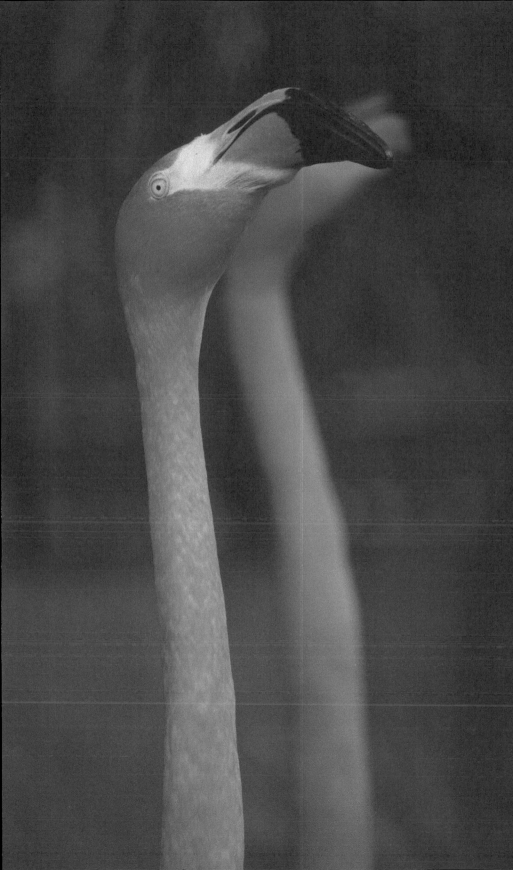

Movement

Flamingos have webbed feet like ducks. This helps them to stand in soft mud and wade through the water to find food.

They can fly up to 35 miles per hour and may fly hundreds of miles in a day.

Flamingos rest by tucking one
leg under their body.

Flamingo Chicks

Before laying an egg, flamingo parents build a mound of dirt and sand to make a nest. The parents take turns sitting on the egg until it hatches. When chicks hatch, they are white and gray in color.

Chicks have down feathers,
which are softer and fluffier
than their parents' feathers.

Life Span

Most flamingos live

between 20 and 30 years

in the wild.

Some flamingos have been

known to live as long as 60

years.

Flamingos are ready to have chicks by the time they are two years old.

Colony Life

Flamingos are very social animals. They live in groups that are called colonies. A colony usually has around 50 birds.

They stay together for social interaction and protection from predators.

Flamingo colonies also work together to keep chicks safe from predators.

Lake Natron

One of the largest colonies of flamingos is found on Lake Natron in Africa. The colony has over one million birds.

It is very hot there and the lake water is very salty. Flamingos are one of the only animals able to live there.

Millions of flamingos fly to Lake

Natron each year to lay eggs.

Population

The greater flamingo has the largest population of any of the six species.

The Andean flamingo of South America is listed as **vulnerable**. It could become **endangered** if the population declines.

Populations of Andean flamingos are getting smaller due to habitat destruction.

Helping Flamingos

Human activities like building roads and mining often disturb or destroy flamingo habitats.

Flamingo habitats can also be disturbed by people who want to come and see wild flamingos.

The Flamingo Specialist Group was founded in 1978 to study and protect wild flamingos.

They work with other groups to help prevent habitat destruction and **conserve** wild flamingo populations.

Glossary

Adapt: to change

Conserve: to keep safe

Crustacean: an animal with a hard shell such as a crab or shrimp

Endangered: at risk of becoming extinct

Migrate: to move from one place to another

Omnivore: an animal that eats plants and other animals

Pigment: the natural color of a part of a plant or animal

Preen: the way a bird cleans its own feathers

Vulnerable: an animal that is likely to become endangered

Widespread: found in a wide area

Wingspan: the distance between the tips of a birds wings

About the Author

Victoria Blakemore is a first grade

teacher in Southwest Florida with a

passion for reading.

You can visit her at

www.elementaryexplorers.com

Also in This Series

Also in This Series